TENNIS

CORGI BOOKS

THE GOLDEN RULES OF TENNIS

A CORGI BOOK 0 552 12595 4

First publication in Great Britain

PRINTING HISTORY
Corgi edition published 1985
Corgi edition reissued 1985

Corgi Books are published by Transworld Publishers Ltd.,
Century House, 61-63 Uxbridge Road, Ealing, London W5 5SA,
in Australia by Transworld Publishers (Aust.) Pty. Ltd.,
26 Harley Crescent, Condell Park, NSW 2200, and in New
Zealand by Transworld Publishers (N.Z.) Ltd., Cnr. Moselle
and Waipareira Avenues, Henderson, Auckland.

Made and printed in Great Britain by
Hunt Barnard Printing Ltd., Aylesbury, Bucks.

Players must be familiar with all the rules of the game.

If they show interest, children should start playing tennis as young as possible.

Ensure you arrive at a match with the right equipment.
Borrowed gear may be ill-fitting or uncomfortable.

5

Clothing should be comfortable and loose-fitting.

When beginning, it is best to practise orthodox shots and not try anything 'flashy'.

Plimsolls or other soft-soled sports shoes only should be worn on court.

Ensure that your racket strings are of the correct tension before going on court.

Never attempt to play tennis unless you are in good physical shape.

The player should endeavour to keep the hair from his eyes, as this could mean lost points, games or even the match.

A headband is useful for keeping long hair away from the eyes.

The choice of ends and the right to be Server or Receiver in the first game shall be decided by the toss of a racket.

To gain the maximum benefit when serving, it is vital to throw the ball high into the air.

The server shall project the ball by hand into the air, unless he has the use of only one arm then he may utilize the racket for the projection.

The service is a fault if the Server misses the ball in attempting to strike it.

The server shall wait until his opponent is ready before delivering the ball.

Endeavour to hit the first serve accurately and with speed.

The position and stance of the Receiver is most important when returning service.

Always be prepared for the unexpected when receiving service.

Always maintain a good firm grip of the racket.

The ball must be struck by the racket.

Practise as much as is possible. If you arrive at the court before your opponent, play a few shots on your own.

When playing in a tournament make sure you understand the committee's ruling on advertising and abide by it.

Always keep your eye on the ball.

When executing a smash you must be perfectly balanced before throwing the racket head at the ball.

The ball must pass OVER the net.

The player must not touch the net with either his racket or any part of his body.

Take extreme care when playing on a wet grass court.

Remember that your judgement may be impaired if the conditions are particularly windy.

The Umpire, in his discretion, may at any time postpone a match on account of the condition of the ground or the weather.

Be prepared for the drop shot. It is deceptive, is hit with backspin and can cause problems to players of all standards.

Wear clothing which is suitable for the weather conditions.

It is advisable to carry a spare racket, especially when playing in a tournament or an important match of any sort.

If standing close to the net make sure that your body is away from the flightpath of the ball or is protected by the racket.

Never keep your opponent waiting when changing ends in a match. You may incur penalties for this at some tournaments.

When playing doubles it is important for both players to decide where to best position themselves.

Play is never delayed to enable a player or players to recover strength or receive advice.

It is courteous to acknowledge a lucky winning shot.

During a match any comments or abuse from the spectators should be ignored by the players.

Ballboys and girls play an important part in a match, and should be treated with the respect they deserve.

If you disagree with a call, have a quiet word with the Umpire and abide by his decision.

Always walk round the net when changing ends. Do not attempt to jump over it.

When playing doubles, decide who will strike the ball if it appears to be going between you.

In some tournaments there is no tie-break in the last set.

Play must not be delayed during doubles matches to discuss tactics or for any other reasons.

Win or lose, it is courteous to shake hands with your opponent or opponents at the end of a match.